Growing
Tomatoes

Growing Tomatoes

WRITER
Philip Hardgrave

PHOTOGRAPHERS
Alan Copeland and
Barry Shapiro

ILLUSTRATOR
James Balkovek

LAWN & GARDEN

Product Manager: CYNTHIA FOLLAND, NK LAWN & GARDEN CO.

Acquisition, Development and Production Services by BMR, Corte Madera, CA

Acquisition: JACK JENNINGS, BOB DOLEZAL

Series Concept: BOB DOLEZAL

Project Director: JANE RYAN

Developmental Editor: JILL FOX

Horticulturist: BARBARA STREMPLE

Photographic Director: ALAN COPELAND

Interior Art Director: BRAD GREENE

Interior Art: JAMES BALKOVEK

NORTH AMERICAN MAP: RON HILDEBRAND

Copy Editor: JANET VOLKMAN

Typography and Page Layout: BARBARA GELFAND

Site Scout: PEGGY HENRY

Photo Assistant: LISA PISCHEL

Cover Design: KAREN EMERSON

Cover Art Director: KARRYLL NASON

Cover Stylist: SUSAN BROUSSARD

Cover Location: ROGERS NK SEED COMPANY, GILROY, CA

Color Separations: PREPRESS ASSEMBLY INCORPORATED

Printing and Binding: PENDELL PRINTING INC.

Production Management: THOMAS E. DORSANEO, JANE RYAN

First Edition

Library of Congress Cataloging-in-Publication Data:
Hardgrave, Phil.
    Growing tomatoes / writer, Phil Hardgrave; photographers, Alan Copeland and Barry Shapiro, illustrator, James Balkovek.
    p. cm. – (NK Lawn & Garden step-by-step visual guide)
Includes index.
    ISBN: 1-880281-06-6
    1. Tomatoes I. Title. II. Series.
SB349.H29 1993
635'.642–dc20   92-20207
                                                CIP

Special thanks to: Drs. John Prendergast, Ray Volin, and Rick Mitchell, Rogers NK Seed Co.; Nancy Peterson; Katherine Kirk; Janet Pischel; Kathie Feidler; Mary Beth and Kurt Reis; Mariam and Dick Dondero; and Robert and Gail Lutolf.

Additional photo credits: Saxon Holt: pgs. 1-9, 18-27, 50-53, 62-67, 72-73

Notice: The information contained in this book is true and complete to the best of our knowledge. All recommendations are made without any guarantees on the part of the authors, NK Lawn & Garden Co., or BMR. Because the means, materials and procedures followed by homeowners are beyond our control, the author and publisher disclaim all liability in connection with the use of this information.

92   93   94   95   10   9   8   7   6   5   4   3   2   1

TABLE OF CONTENTS

GETTING STARTED

Garden fresh tomatoes are wonderful to eat and easy to grow. Start early in the season, plant your seeds at the right time, cultivate them properly, and you can grow delicious tomatoes no matter where you live.

GROWING TOMATOES

The tomato plant is undoubtedly the most widely grown vegetable in America, and harvesting its fruit is the ambition of nearly every beginning gardener. The enormous appeal of garden fresh tomatoes is not hard to understand: they are easy to grow, take up little space and require relatively little work to produce a big harvest of delicious fruit.

There are only a few basic requirements for growing tomatoes: a minimum of six hours of sun each day in summer, a slow but steady supply of water and the proper soil structure and nutrients.

The tomato is a warm-season plant, but the development of improved varieties for cooler areas allows home gardeners from virtually any climate zone to grow some type of tomato. These specially cultivated varieties, called cultivars, are bred by growers for specific pest and disease resistance, climate conditions and growing seasons.

Fresh slicing tomatoes are those you pick and eat immediately. While these are a universal favorite, tomatoes are also well suited for canning, freezing and drying. The reward of home growing is an explosion of rich tomato flavor that the store-bought, shelf-ripened varieties can never offer. As easy as it is to grow tomatoes, some of the best gardeners seem to have trouble, probably because they assume that tomatoes require no care at all. If the soil and site conditions happen to be right, and you have a lot of luck, tomato plants can grow forgotten and uncared for and produce a crop of fruit, but the guarantee of a great harvest is proper feeding, watering and protection from pests, diseases and weather damage.

EVERYONE'S FAVORITE FRUIT

Used in salads, juices, appetizers, sauces and preserves, tomatoes are the most versatile fruit in the garden. They come in many shapes, sizes and colors, so enjoy experimenting with different varieties.

SPECIALTY TOMATOES Exotic varieties with unusual marbling, stripes or skin texture.

HYBRIDS Improved cultivars created by cross-pollinating two standard varieties for disease resistance and other traits.

PEARS AND PLUMS Small, meaty tomatoes better suited for pastes, sauces or preserving.

CHERRIES Bite-sized miniatures for use in salads and as individual appetizers.

YELLOW, PINK AND WHITE Colorful varieties add excitement to your garden and table.

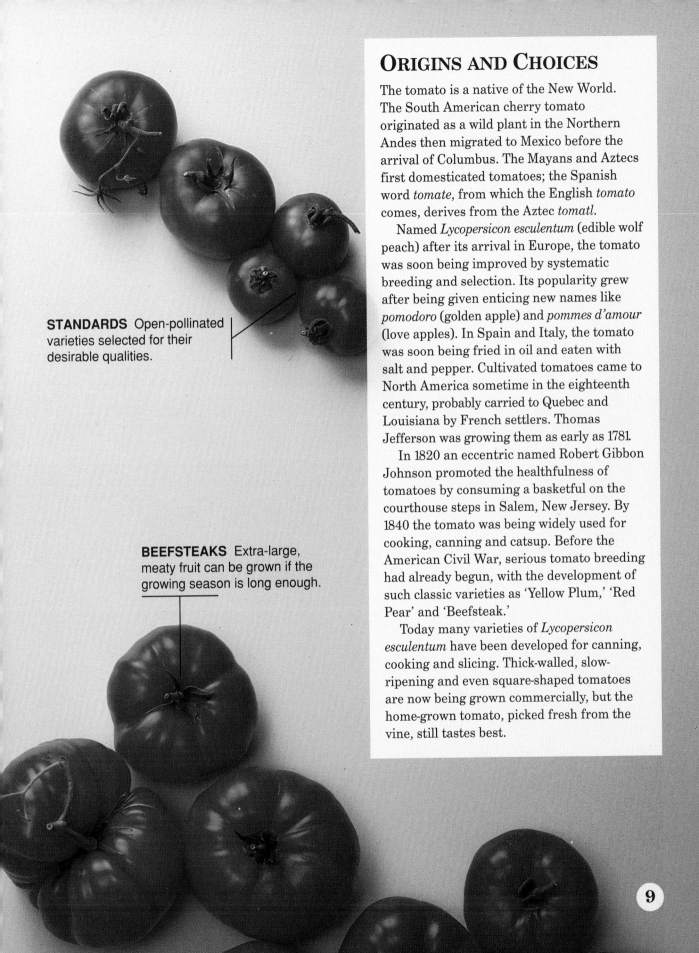

STANDARDS Open-pollinated varieties selected for their desirable qualities.

BEEFSTEAKS Extra-large, meaty fruit can be grown if the growing season is long enough.

ORIGINS AND CHOICES

The tomato is a native of the New World. The South American cherry tomato originated as a wild plant in the Northern Andes then migrated to Mexico before the arrival of Columbus. The Mayans and Aztecs first domesticated tomatoes; the Spanish word *tomate*, from which the English *tomato* comes, derives from the Aztec *tomatl*.

Named *Lycopersicon esculentum* (edible wolf peach) after its arrival in Europe, the tomato was soon being improved by systematic breeding and selection. Its popularity grew after being given enticing new names like *pomodoro* (golden apple) and *pommes d'amour* (love apples). In Spain and Italy, the tomato was soon being fried in oil and eaten with salt and pepper. Cultivated tomatoes came to North America sometime in the eighteenth century, probably carried to Quebec and Louisiana by French settlers. Thomas Jefferson was growing them as early as 1781.

In 1820 an eccentric named Robert Gibbon Johnson promoted the healthfulness of tomatoes by consuming a basketful on the courthouse steps in Salem, New Jersey. By 1840 the tomato was being widely used for cooking, canning and catsup. Before the American Civil War, serious tomato breeding had already begun, with the development of such classic varieties as 'Yellow Plum,' 'Red Pear' and 'Beefsteak.'

Today many varieties of *Lycopersicon esculentum* have been developed for canning, cooking and slicing. Thick-walled, slow-ripening and even square-shaped tomatoes are now being grown commercially, but the home-grown tomato, picked fresh from the vine, still tastes best.

When to Plant Tomatoes

Finding Your Climate Zone

The climate zone map is a general guide to the predicted dates of the last frost in spring and the first frost in autumn; this tells the approximate length of the outdoor growing season for tomatoes in each area. To use the map, find your location and its zone color, then look up the earliest planting dates for that zone. Some newer tomato cultivars have been bred specifically for extreme climates. For most older varieties, the number of days from transplanting to maturity will indicate whether you can grow that tomato to full ripeness in your area.

Although more detailed climate maps can provide useful information on average annual minimum temperature, average soil temperature and average length of growing season, these averages are not absolutes for any particular place—the actual conditions for your garden may vary considerably. The microclimate in your immediate area, affected by hills, valleys, sunlight and shadows, could be as much as an entire zone off from the surrounding region.

Always consult your local nursery or county Agricultural Extension Service about the growing season in your neighborhood. Study the conditions in your garden that might affect when to plant your tomatoes.

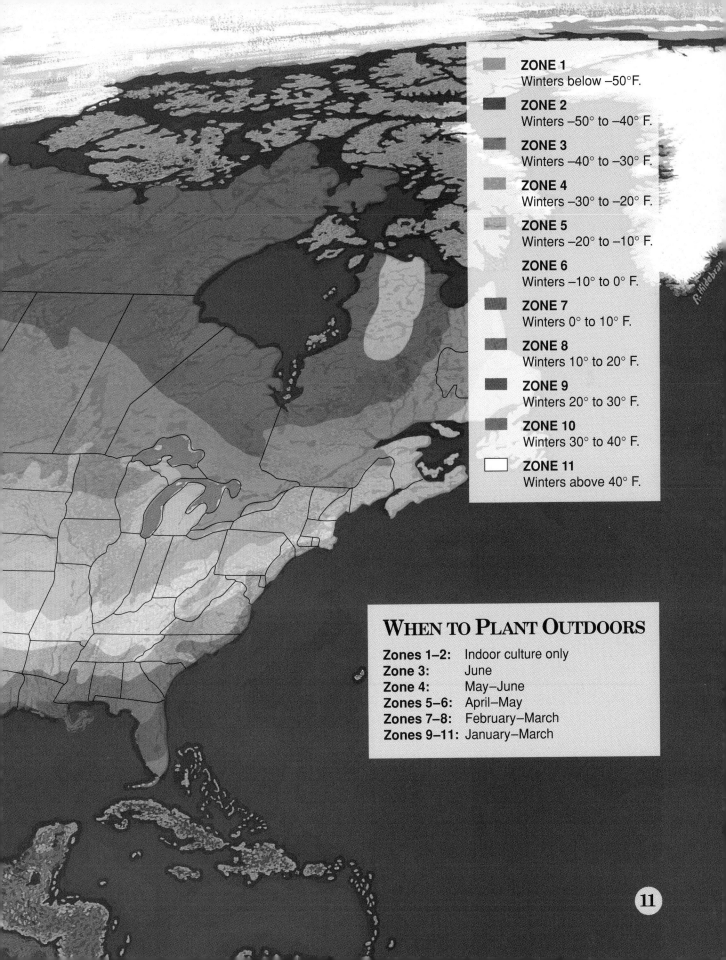

ZONE 1
Winters below −50°F.

ZONE 2
Winters −50° to −40° F.

ZONE 3
Winters −40° to −30° F.

ZONE 4
Winters −30° to −20° F.

ZONE 5
Winters −20° to −10° F.

ZONE 6
Winters −10° to 0° F.

ZONE 7
Winters 0° to 10° F.

ZONE 8
Winters 10° to 20° F.

ZONE 9
Winters 20° to 30° F.

ZONE 10
Winters 30° to 40° F.

ZONE 11
Winters above 40° F.

WHEN TO PLANT OUTDOORS

Zones 1–2: Indoor culture only
Zone 3: June
Zone 4: May–June
Zones 5–6: April–May
Zones 7–8: February–March
Zones 9–11: January–March

WHERE TO PLANT TOMATOES

CHOOSING A GARDEN SITE

The ideal tomato garden site will have full sun through most of the day, shelter from the wind and easy access to water. Tomatoes can be grown in containers or in a spot by a fence, wall or side of the house, but open sites are best. Try to choose a place with good southern or southeastern exposure and avoid poorly drained areas.

To find a good garden location, look for a place with loose, loamy soil. Avoid setting the new garden under trees or next to shrubs that will compete with your tomatoes for sunlight, water and soil nutrients. If temperature extremes or high winds are a common occurrence in your area, place the bed in a well protected spot with a natural or man-made windbreak, such as a house, high wall or screening row of trees.

Space is rarely a problem because you don't need many plants; a half-dozen prolific tomato plants can supply an entire family with all the fruit they will need for the year. Even larger plants only need between four to six square feet of growing room, depending on the variety. Leave enough room between plants for water lines, trellises or wire supports you may want to add later and for moving around and between plants when gardening.

HILLSIDE WITH STAKES If a terrace has good drainage, full sun and a southward slope, tomatoes will do well there.

PATIOS One- to five-gallon planters or barrels make excellent container gardens.

GARDEN Any sunny location with workable soil and good drainage can be used to grow tomatoes.

GREENHOUSE WINDOW
A sunny windowsill or greenhouse window can be a good spot for starting seeds indoors.

DECKS Be sure the deck structure can support the weight of the container, soil and plants.

KITCHEN GARDEN Plan to grow herbs and other vegetables near the kitchen for convenience.

13

HOW TOMATOES GROW

Most tomato plants look alike from a distance, but there are two types of tomato plants, determinate and indeterminate, grown for different reasons. Note the various parts of the plant and the roles they play in plant growth and fruit development.

RIPE FRUIT Pick vine-ripened fruit when it has a bright color and the flesh softens slightly.

BUDS Each bud should blossom, pollinate, and then set fruit.

STEMS Sturdy stems carry water and nutrients to the plant. Buried stems will grow new roots.

BLOSSOMS Petals, stigma, pistil and pollen all play a role in fruit production.

MAGNIFIED FLOWER PART

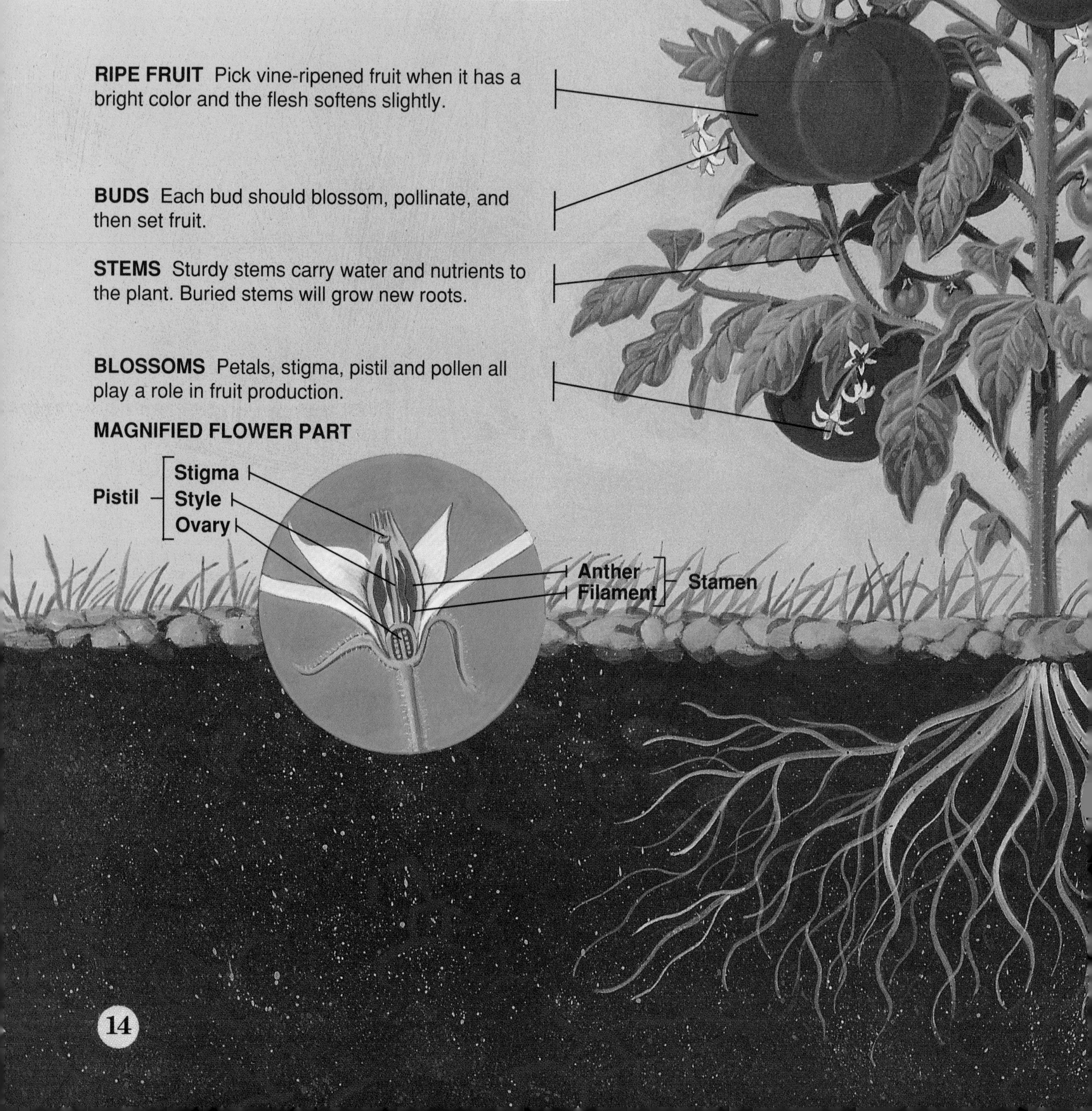

Pistil
- Stigma
- Style
- Ovary

Anther
Filament
Stamen

LEAVES Green leaves perform the vital function of photosynthesis and protect fruit from summer sun.

NEW FRUIT Fruit sets and grows for a month or more and then ripens for harvest.

ROOT SYSTEM Healthy roots absorb moisture and nutrients and anchor the plant in the ground.

TWO PLANT TYPES

Determinate tomato plants reach a fixed full size, after which buds develop at the tips and the branches stop growing. All flowers blossom around the same time and set fruit in clusters, within a one- or two-week period. Because the fruit ripens all at once, determinate tomatoes are best for preserving; otherwise, most of the home harvest may spoil before it can be eaten.

Indeterminate tomato plants grow like vines, reaching higher and higher until pulled up or killed by frost. Blossoms set fruit along side branches while the plant continues to grow. With their fruit in various stages of maturity as the harvest begins, indeterminate tomatoes can be picked over a long period of time.

BEFORE YOU BUY

SEED OR TRANSPLANT?

Transplanting from commercially sold six-packs or four-inch pots is the quickest way to get plants into the ground, but growing from seeds is less expensive and can be an educational and enjoyable family activity. Starting seeds indoors gives you greater control over the variety selection, growing season, soil conditions and temperature. You can grow under lights or in a sunny window.

Allow four to five weeks, sometimes more, for seedlings to develop to the four to six inch size suitable for transplanting. Starting earlier and growing plants to a larger size indoors won't guarantee a huge increase in final plant size or fruit yield, but it may help lengthen the growing season for maximum ripeness. Planting seeds in pairs allows you to select only the strongest seedlings.

Before the seedlings are ready to be transplanted outdoors, prepare the garden soil well (see pg. 28). Remember to keep your plants labeled with the variety and the dates of sowing and transplanting.

Sowing from seeds offers the home grower access to varieties not commonly found in nurseries. The seed packet tells you regions in which the variety grows best, whether the plant is determinate or indeterminate, the number of days to maturity, the feeding requirements, growth characteristics, uses and disease tolerance and resistance of the tomato.

STERILIZED POTTING MIX Ensures that no soil pests or diseases are transmitted to new plants.

ORGANIC POTTING SOIL
An All Purpose Transplanting Mix

SEEDING FLATS One large tray or many individual sections for growing plants from seeds.

SEED PACKETS Save to identify the variety and growing characteristics of each plant.

DISEASE TOLERANCE AND RESISTANCE

One of the surest ways to achieve a virgorous tomato crop is to grow plants tolerant of and resistant to disease. Disease tolerance and disease resistance have different meanings. Many newer varieties of tomatoes are genetically bred to be *resistant* to the most common diseases, such as verticillium wilt, fusarium wilt, nematodes or tobacco mosaic virus (see pg. 60). These varieties are identified with the letters V, F, N or T, indicating that they have been developed from generations of plants that have resisted those diseases. Newer varieties may distinguish between the two most common fusarium races, 1 and 2; those resisting both species are dubbed 1 and 2, and their seed packs marked "VFFNT." Resistance to *Alternaria* leaf spot is indicated by the letter A.

Disease *tolerance* is the ability to withstand diseases once they have developed; a disease-tolerant plant may be infected or infested, but not destroyed, by the offending organism. Familiarize yourself with the range of pests and diseases affecting your garden and choose varieties accordingly. Mulching, applying fungicides and pesticides and feeding are other ways to help tomato plants combat disease.

PEAT POTS Seeding containers that can go directly into the ground later.

SIX PACK PLANTS Always inspect for disease or pest problems before purchasing.

GARDEN TOOLS Good tools make garden work easier, indoor or out; a complete list of tools appears on pg. 34.

Choosing Early-Season Slicing Tomatoes

Early season tomatoes take 66 days or less from transplanting to maturity; they can produce an early harvest for anyone anxious for their first tomato, but they are especially helpful in colder climates where the growing season is short.

QUICK PICK HYBRID Excellent disease resistance and meaty texture recommend this popular variety.

MERCED HYBRID Deep red, firm flesh with strong disease resistance.

EARLY GIRL IMPROVED HYBRID Reliable in northern climates, this tomato has great taste and resists cracking and disease well.

Cultivar	Days to Fruit	Plant Type	Fruit Size (oz.)	Disease Resistance	Comments
Burpeeana Early Hybrid	58	I	5		Mild-flavored, high fruit yields
Burpee's Early Pick Hybrid	62	I	8	VF	Good disease and cold resistance
Burpee's Big Early Hybrid	62	I	8		Thick-walled fruit, cage or trellis support
Bush Beefsteak	62	D	8		Compact, high yield, good northern grower
Champion Hybrid	62	I	10	VFNT	Long harvest, good flavor; tolerates hot weather
Earliana	58	I	5–6		Mild-flavored fruit, bright red color
Earlirouge	63	D	6–7	V	Sweet fruit, tolerates temperature extremes
Early Cascade Hybrid	55	I	5	VF	Late harvest, high yield; staked or caged
Early Girl Improved Hybrid	54	I	4–6	VFF	Harvest summer to fall, staked or caged
First Lady Hybrid	66	I	4–6	VFNT	Disease resistance, needs staking or caging
Good 'n' Early Hybrid	62	I	7	VFT	Good yields and rich flavor
Merced Hybrid	65	D	9	VFFT	Excellent early season variety
Oregon Spring	58	D	10	V	Good for areas with short growing season
Quick Pick Hybrid	60	I	5	VFNTA	Good disease resistance
Springset Hybrid	65	D	6	VF	Heavy yield, quick harvest; grow in cages
Sub-arctic Maxi	62	D	2–3		Far north favorite, good yield and taste

D=Determinate plant   I=Indeterminate plant   V=Verticillium wilt   F=Fusarium wilt   N=Nematodes   T=Tobacco mosaic virus   A=Alternaria

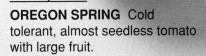

OREGON SPRING Cold tolerant, almost seedless tomato with large fruit.

FIRST LADY HYBRID An improved version of Early Girl, this plant is highly disease resistant with smooth, flavorful fruit.

CHOOSING MID-SEASON SLICING TOMATOES

Mid-season tomatoes are the varieties that take between 66 and 80 days from transplanting to maturity. Sometimes called *main crop* tomatoes, they are generally larger and juicier than the early-season varieties.

PATIO HYBRID An excellent choice for small gardens or containers.

ACE 55 Produces fruit resistant to verticillium and fusarium wilt.

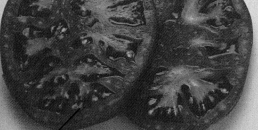

CELEBRITY HYBRID Popular disease resistant variety, sets fruit in all climate zones.

BEEF KING HYBRID Big, beefy one pound fruit on a disease-resistant plant.

BETTER BOY HYBRID A favorite all-purpose variety is highly reliable with unlimited size and yields.

KING'S CHOICE HYBRID Delivers rich, meaty fruit all season long with excellent disease resistance.

FLAVOR KING HYBRID Super-sweet medium-sized fruit, resists cracking and diseases.

Cultivar	Days to Fruit	Plant Type	Fruit Size (oz.)	Disease Resistance	Comments
Ace 55	80	D	10	VF	Good disease resistance
Beef King Hybrid	70	I	16	VFNA	Resists disease well for a beefsteak type
Better Boy Hybrid	72	I	16	VFNA	Popular large slicer, grows in hot and cold climates
Better Bush Hybrid	78	I	8	VFN	Outstanding yield from a 3 ft. plant
Big Pick Hybrid	70	I	12–16	VFFNTA	Superb disease resistance, caged or staked
Big Set Hybrid	75	D	9	VFN	Early mid-season harvest, outstanding disease resistance
Burpee's Big Boy Hybrid	78	I	16		Old favorite, benefits from caging
Burpee's Big Girl Hybrid	78	I	12	VF	Improved Big Boy, less cracking
Carnival Hybrid	70	D	8	VFFNT	Celebrity type with earlier fruit
Celebrity Hybrid	70	D	8	VFFNTA	Thin-skinned, high-yield fruit; outstanding disease resistance
Fantastic Hybrid	72	I	6–8		Long harvest, sets fruit in hot or cold weather
Flavor King Hybrid	70	I	7	VFFT	Sweet, crack resistant, staked or caged
Floramerica Hybrid	75	D	8–10	VFF	Widely adapted, good choice for humid climates
Heartland Hybrid	68	I	6–8	VFN	Improved container type with full-sized fruit
King's Choice Hybrid	70	I	10–14	VFFNT	Long harvest, deep red fruit, strong disease resistance
Lady Luck Hybrid	78	I	16	VFNT	Big fruit, wide spectrum disease resistance
Marglobe Improved	75	D	6	VF	Old-fashioned with improved VF resistance
Mountain Pride Hybrid	74	D	6	VFFA	Big globe-shaped, green-shouldered fruit
Patio Hybrid	70	D	4–6	F	Compact growth habit; requires little growing space
President Hybrid	68	D	12–16	VFFNT	Meaty fruit, disease resistant
Super Fantastic Hybrid	70	I	10	VFN	Improved Fantastic, very high yields
Terrific Hybrid	70	I	8–10	VFNTA	Superb taste, good disease resistance

D=Determinate plant   I=Indeterminate plant   V=Verticillium wilt   F=Fusarium wilt   N=Nematodes   T=Tobacco mosaic virus   A=Alternaria

CHOOSING LATE-SEASON SLICING TOMATOES

Late season varieties, including most of the giant 'Beefsteak' tomatoes, take 80 days or more from transplanting to harvest. Combining early, mid-season, and late varieties will provide the longest harvest period for your garden.

HOMESTEAD 24 Southeastern favorite, with thick-walled fruit that resists heat and sunscalding problems well.

SUPER BUSH HYBRID An excellent choice for containers and small spaces, giving a long harvest of juicy 4–5 oz. fruit.

Variety	Days to Fruit	Plant Type	Fruit Size (oz.)	Disease Resistance	Comments
Ace	85	I	8–12	VF	Smooth skin, high yield
Beefmaster Hybrid	80	I	20	VFN	Widely adapted, good disease resistance
Beefsteak	90	I	14		Big, sweet one pound fruit
Burpee's Supersteak Hybrid	80	I	18–20	VFN	Good for slicing, disease resistant
Cal-Ace	80	D	10	VF	Sets fruit in very hot weather
Climbing Trip-L-Crop	90	I	16		Giant plant, heavy yields
Giant Tree	88	I	6–8		Old-fashioned climbing plant
Glamour	88	I	5		Crack resistant, needs caging
Homestead 24	80	D	8	F	Good tropical climate plant, withstands humidity
Manalucie	80	I	8	F	Southeast favorite, crack and rot tolerant
Oxheart	80	I	16–24		Unique heart shape, needs caging
Super Bush Hybrid	80	D	5	VFN	Good container plant, long harvest
Tropic	80	I	10–12	VFT	Greenhouse type, super disease resistance
Wonder Boy Hybrid	80	I	8	VFN	Heavy yields, hot weather plant

D=Determinate plant   I=Indeterminate plant   V=Verticillium wilt   F=Fusarium wilt   N=Nematodes   T=Tobacco mosaic virus   A=Alternaria

BEEFSTEAK The old-fashioned standard for this type, with big, fleshy fruit on large cores.

ACE A popular home selection for its pleasant, mild taste.

BEEFMASTER HYBRID Good disease resistance for a beefsteak type; its vigorous growth often needs caging.

CHOOSING MINIATURE TOMATOES

Miniature tomatoes grow on both full-sized and dwarf plants. Choose varieties that grow to a smaller plant size—some have vines as short as 4 inches at maturity—for container gardening and when space is limited.

GOLD NUGGET Compact plant with mild, seedless fruit.

SUPER SWEET 100 HYBRID Produces big clusters of many sweet-flavored 1 1/4 in. fruit in 65–70 days, with a long harvest.

CHERRY KING HYBRID Produces season-long harvests of firm, 1 1/2 in. fruit with a deep red color.

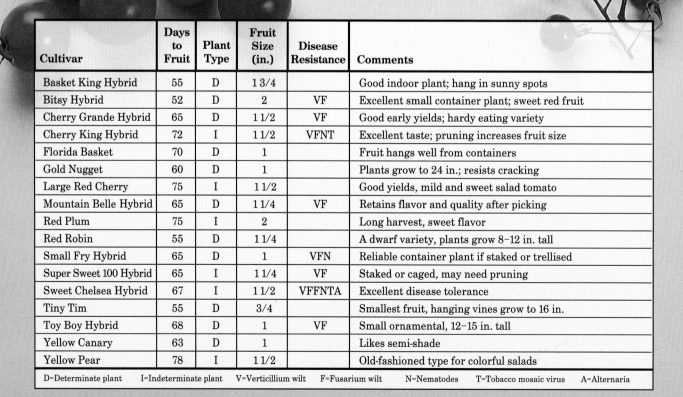

Cultivar	Days to Fruit	Plant Type	Fruit Size (in.)	Disease Resistance	Comments
Basket King Hybrid	55	D	1 3/4		Good indoor plant; hang in sunny spots
Bitsy Hybrid	52	D	2	VF	Excellent small container plant; sweet red fruit
Cherry Grande Hybrid	65	D	1 1/2	VF	Good early yields; hardy eating variety
Cherry King Hybrid	72	I	1 1/2	VFNT	Excellent taste; pruning increases fruit size
Florida Basket	70	D	1		Fruit hangs well from containers
Gold Nugget	60	D	1		Plants grow to 24 in.; resists cracking
Large Red Cherry	75	I	1 1/2		Good yields, mild and sweet salad tomato
Mountain Belle Hybrid	65	D	1 1/4	VF	Retains flavor and quality after picking
Red Plum	75	I	2		Long harvest, sweet flavor
Red Robin	55	D	1 1/4		A dwarf variety, plants grow 8–12 in. tall
Small Fry Hybrid	65	D	1	VFN	Reliable container plant if staked or trellised
Super Sweet 100 Hybrid	65	I	1 1/4	VF	Staked or caged, may need pruning
Sweet Chelsea Hybrid	67	I	1 1/2	VFFNTA	Excellent disease tolerance
Tiny Tim	55	D	3/4		Smallest fruit, hanging vines grow to 16 in.
Toy Boy Hybrid	68	D	1	VF	Small ornamental, 12–15 in. tall
Yellow Canary	63	D	1		Likes semi-shade
Yellow Pear	78	I	1 1/2		Old-fashioned type for colorful salads

D=Determinate plant   I=Indeterminate plant   V=Verticillium wilt   F=Fusarium wilt   N=Nematodes   T=Tobacco mosaic virus   A=Alternaria

MOUNTAIN BELLE HYBRID
High yields of bright red cherry
fruit resists cracking.

YELLOW PEAR Brilliant yellow
1 1/2 in. pear-shaped fruit are
good for preserving or as salad
garnish.

RED ROBIN Excellent for
container and patio plantings.

CONTAINER CHOICES

Tomatoes can be grown successfully in containers on decks and patios, in window boxes and even in hanging baskets and pots. If you don't have workable soil or enough space for a tomato garden, consider the many options presented by container growing.

Use the chart to find which varieties are particularly recommended for baskets, planters or pots. The name and fruit size often indicate whether the plant is best suited for an indoor container or should be placed outdoors in a larger planter. Remember that lack of pollination and fruit set can be a problem with isolated container plants (see pg. 62). You will be more successful grouping several containers in one area. Check the seed packet for individual growing directions.

Many advocates of container growing preach the virtues of five-gallon buckets and big wooden barrels, but miniature tomatoes can be grown in one-gallon baskets if properly watered and fertilized. Larger pots will typically enhance the size and fruit yield of plants. You can grow tomatoes in wood, plastic or clay containers; just be sure they drain well. Install one plant in each container, rather than several plants in a large container. Individual containers will usually produce more fruit than a single big planter box arrangement.

Containers let you experiment with planter design and display. A nicely made trellis or A-frame rack attached to a container can prove a handsome addition to even a small deck or patio. Set containers on risers to provide easy access, an important consideration if age or handicap makes working at ground level difficult.

The steps for growing tomatoes in containers are the same as for growing them in the ground, generally. The special needs of growing in containers are discussed on pgs. 44–45.

CHOOSING PRESERVING AND PASTE TOMATOES

Many tomatoes have been specially developed for preserving and making paste. Any firm, fleshy tomato can be preserved by freezing or canning; small, meaty tomatoes are best for cooking into sauce or paste.

ROMA This popular egg-shaped tomato used for paste can also be eaten fresh in salads or sautéed and served over pasta.

LA ROSSA HYBRID A common preserving variety with rich red color.

Variety	Days to Fruit	Plant Type	Fruit Size	Disease Resistance	Comments
PRESERVING					
La Rossa Hybrid	76	D	3 1/2 in.	VFF	All-purpose preserving tomato, thick-walled
Milano Hybrid	78	D	3 in.	VFF	Pear-shaped paste tomato, sweet with uniform size
San Marzano	80	D	3 1/2 in.		Classic rectangular shaped paste and canning tomato
Roma	75	D	3	VF	Best-known paste tomato, rich flavor and color
Super Italian Paste	70	I	6 in.		Large fruit, very meaty with few seeds
Viva Italia Hybrid	80	D	3 in.	VFN	More disease resistant than Roma or San Marzano
HUSK TOMATOES					
Ground Cherry	80		1/2 in.		Used for preserves and pies
Tomatillo	95		1 1/2 in.		Ripening fruit turns yellow but is best eaten green
NOVELTY					
Golden Boy Hybrid	80	I	8–10 oz.		The only yellow hybrid, large mild fruit
Jubilee	80	I	8 oz.		Burpee's All-America, big smooth yellow-orange fruit
Lemon Boy Hybrid	72	D	7 oz.	VFN	Lemon yellow globe-shaped fruit for ornament or salad
Pink Girl Hybrid	76	I	7–8 oz.	VFA	Globe-shaped fruit resists cracking well
Pink Ponderosa	80	I	12–24 oz.		Pink-skinned cultivar of classic beefsteak

D=Determinate plant   I=Indeterminate plant   V=Verticillium wilt   F=Fusarium wilt   N=Nematodes   T=Tobacco mosaic virus   A=Alternaria

VIVA ITALIA HYBRID High-sugar hybrid combines disease resistance with good hot weather fruit-setting.

SUPER ITALIAN PASTE
Heirloom variety, 2–3 times larger than common paste tomatoes.

HUSK TOMATOES

Tomatoes belong to the important nightshade family, which includes peppers, eggplants, potatoes and a number of popular ornamental plants. Other plants are sometimes called tomatoes, or husk tomatoes, although they are not tomatoes. Their leaves, flowers and fruit are very different upon closer inspection. The tomatillo (*Physalis ixocarpa*) is an annual that bears a green, spicy-tasting 1/2–3/4 inch fruit used in many Mexican dishes, most notably *salsa verde*. Another husk tomato, the ground cherry (*Physalis pruinosa*), is a member of the nightshade family but not a true tomato. Its sweet, greenish-yellow 1/2–3/4 inch fruit are used in pies and jams.

Novelty tomatoes, bred for their unusual color, shape or skin texture, often don't look like tomatoes at first glance. Yellow tomatoes really are yellow inside, but pink tomatoes have red meat that looks pink because the skin is translucent. Commercial growers have developed square-shaped tomatoes for packing purposes; like the exotic striped and marbled varieties, these are rarely available as store-bought plants. Peach-skin tomatoes are likewise difficult to find. Unlike tomatillos and ground cherries, however, these unusual varieties are all true tomatoes under the skin.

PREPARING THE SOIL

GOOD TOMATO SOIL

The ideal tomato soil has a porous, crumbly texture, an abundance of nutrients, and no pests or diseases present. Use any good sterile potting soil in containers. A good choice is potting soil mixed with materials such as perlite, peat moss, vermiculite or sand, which is sold under many brand names in nurseries and garden centers.

The soil in containers requires better drainage and heavier feeding than outdoor garden soils; frequent watering and quick drainage leaches out soil nutrients. Steady feeding is needed to replace quickly lost nitrogen, which is essential to leaf development and plant growth. Phosphorus, potassium and the various micronutrients need less frequent application.

A well-balanced, slightly acid mixture of clay, silt and sand particles makes a good outdoor garden soil. Tomatoes can grow in heavy clay soil if it is well drained, but loose, sandy loam is preferable. Adding about one-third organic matter to the garden soil will supply nutrients essential to growth and improve soil structure.

RAISED BED MATERIALS

Garden lime for marking	2 x 12 in. untreated redwood or cedar boards (measure linear feet of bed perimeter)
Spade or shovel	
Rake	
Wheelbarrow	1 x 3 in. 2-ft. redwood or cedar stakes (2 per corner plus 1 each 16 in. around perimeter)
1/4 x 3 in. lag screws (2 per stake plus 3 per corner)	

Building a Raised Bed

First Choose site. Mark border with garden lime.

Then Dig 2-in. trench along marked border. Loosen soil or remove top 18 in. for replacement.

Next Place edge of boards in trench. Drive stakes every 16 in. on inside, fasten lag screws.

Last Add soil amendments. Dig 8–24 in. to mix with soil, rake smooth.

Double-Digging

First Choose site. Mark area with garden lime.

Then Dig trench 8 in. deep to the edge of the bed and set aside soil. Loosen subsoil another 8–10 in.

Next Mix 2–4 in. of amendments to set-aside soil.

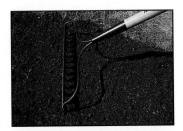

Last Return amended soil to the trench, rake and level. Repeat down the length of the bed.

IMPROVING SOIL

Before planting, it is a good idea to check the pH, fertility and drainage of your soil. A pH test measures acidity on a scale of 0 (acid) to 14 (alkaline); pH 7.0 is neutral. Tomatoes can grow in soil from pH 5.5 to 7.5, but like most other vegetables, they prefer a slightly acid pH of 6.0–6.8. There should be enough calcium to prevent blossom end rot (see pg. 63) and adequate nitrogen, phosphorus and potassium. Use a home test kit to measure soil fertility and pH, or send a sample to your nursery or county extension service for testing. The results will explain the soil amendments you need to add to improve the soil.

Tomatoes grow best in soil that drains well. To test drainage, dig a hole of one cubic foot, fill it with water, then time how long it takes the water to soak in completely. A good loamy soil should drain in 5–15 minutes.

To build up the garden soil, first cultivate to the desired depth, then spread organic compost or other soil amendments at least two to four inches deep across the garden bed. A raised-bed garden may only require digging and turning the soil down to about 18 inches; a new row garden will benefit from double-digging down to 24 inches or more. Level the soil, break up any large clods and rake the surface smooth for planting.

CAUTION

Never use preservative-treated lumber for vegetable gardens.

STARTING SEEDS INDOORS

Starting tomato seeds is easy and enjoyable. Sow your seeds four to five weeks before the last predicted frost in your area. Give them a week or so to germinate and another month to reach the four to six inch size suitable for transplanting outdoors.

First Fill sterile soil mix to within 1/2 in. of top of container; soil must be kept between 70–80°F for germination.

Seeds can be started in almost any clean container—flats, peat pots, peat pellets, egg cartons, even tin cans or 4-in. pots to avoid intermediate transfer.

Then Water lightly and allow to drain. Poke small holes in soil 1–2 in. apart or dig 1/4–in. deep furrows in open flats, spacing furrows 2–3 in. apart.

A sunny windowsill or greenhouse window is a good warm place to start seeds. You can start seeds anywhere if you set containers under grow lights for a maximum of 12 hours each day.

Or Set peat pots or pellets on a tray and fill tray with water. Peat pots will absorb water; keep them damp during germination. Place seeds in peat pots or pellets after they are fully extended.

Third If starting seeds in flats, place 2 seeds together 1–2 in. apart in furrow. Later you will eliminate the weaker seedling if both germinate.

Fourth Use your fingers to cover the seeds and lightly firm the soil around the seeds.

Fifth Water the soil in container or flat gently to keep seeds moist during germination.

Sixth Cover the seedling container with plastic to retain soil moisture; plastic should not touch soil. Poke small holes in plastic.

Seventh When sprouts appear, remove the plastic immediately. Keep container at 60–70°F, in a well-lit location. If both seeds sprout, use scissors to snip off weaker seedling.

Last Once the second set of true leaves appear, transfer seedlings grown in smaller containers into 4-in. pots. Unlike smooth-edged seedling leaves, true leaves have rippled edges.

GROWING SEEDLINGS FOR TRANSPLANT

Growing tomato seedlings is not difficult if a few common problems are avoided. Getting seedlings to the transplanting stage requires consistent moisture, light and warmth and your careful assistance in culling out weaker plants.

Damping Off Fungus can kill stems of seedlings or young plants at the soil line. Planting seeds on sterilized soil can help to prevent damping off. After seeds are planted, avoid over-watering and keep soil temperature between 70–80°F until germination.

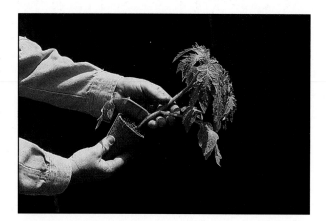

Ready to Transplant Outdoors Whether grown from seed or purchased from a nursery or garden center, the ideal transplant is 4–6 in. tall, with a stocky stem and a well-developed second pair of true leaves. These transplants are hardy enough to ward off many of the threats to a successful plant, such as pests, diseases and weeds. Avoid plants that show signs of damping off, weak or leggy stems, yellow leaves or wilting as shown in these photos.

Weak Stems Strengthen stems by pinching off the tip of the seedling, letting side branches develop as the stem gets stocky. When transferring seedlings with weak stems to a larger pot, bury plant up to first true leaves for best results.

Leggy Seedling Tomatoes root off their stems. Remove lower leaves of weak and leggy plants, bury the stem to the first true leaves and roots will grow along the buried portion of the stem.

Yellow Leaves Poor soil nutrients may require addition of nitrogen or chelated iron. Over-watering can also cause yellow leaves.

Wilting Check soil moisture for dry rootball; look for signs of wilt disease, support stem with small stake and string.

PREVENTING PROBLEMS

Young seedlings are particularly susceptible to the effects of temperature, soil moisture and light. For best results, make sure the container is kept warm and the soil damp after the seeds are planted. Keep the soil temperature 70–80°F until germination; never let the soil dry out during this period. Covering seed trays loosely with clear plastic will ensure good moisture retention. Warmth, not light, is needed for seed germination.

Once seedlings appear, expose them to sunlight or overhead grow lights for as long as possible, up to a maximum of 12 hours each day. Use commercial grow lights or combine fluorescent and incandescent lights to get the ideal full spectrum of light; keep fluorescent lamps about six inches from the plants and hot incandescent lights farther away. Raise overhead lights as the seedlings grow to avoid burning the young plant leaves.

Seedlings prefer daytime temperatures of 65–75°F. Turn lights off and let the nighttime temperature cool off to 55–65°F to acclimate the young plants to the day-night cycle.

Leggy, weak-stemmed or deformed seedlings should be thinned out immediately; always start more seedlings than you need for your garden, so that you can cut off the weaklings. When the stronger seedlings develop their second pair of true leaves at about three to four inches in height, repot them into four-inch containers and start to prepare them for the move outdoors.

TOOLS AND EQUIPMENT

Buying and using the right tool for the job saves you time and effort when gardening. Always clean and store tools carefully, and know which tool is designed for each gardening chore.

Weeding Tool

Hand Trowel

Spade

Garden Hoe

Rotary Tiller

Watering Can

Hose and Soaker

Supports

Cultivator

Garden Shovel

Supports

Garden Rake

SELECTION AND CARE

Gardening tools should be sturdy and comfortable. Try out tools for fit and feel before buying—they come in a wide variety of sizes, weights and prices. A well-made work tool will pay for itself many times over in ease of use and provide years of good service. Check for solid construction and materials, whether wood, plastic or steel, and avoid tools that are obviously flimsy, even if they seem like a bargain.

The decision to rent or buy tools boils down to a matter of cost versus convenience. Large, expensive equipment that is used only rarely, such as a rotary tiller, should probably be rented, unless you have enough storage space and regular garden work to justify a considerable investment.

Clean and care for your tools after each work session, removing soil and debris. Store them in a dry place over the winter. Wipe all steel and iron surfaces with light machine oil to avoid rust corrosion problems. Keep your garden tools in good order inside the storage area; this will save valuable time when you go looking for a tool that you suddenly need many months later.

BUILDING A COLDFRAME

Give tomatoes an early start in cold climates by using this easy-to-build coldframe. A coldframe is a miniature greenhouse that keeps transplants warmly insulated when daytime temperatures are still below 70°F, or nighttime temperatures drop below 50°F.

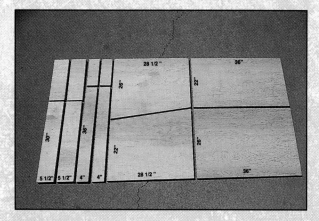

First Carefully cut plywood into pieces of size and shape shown. Cut 1/2 in. edge slot in 5 1/2 x 30 in. pieces for corrugated fiber glass, using table saw blade. Set aside with 4 x 36 in. strips for later use in making cover.

Next Fit fiber glass into slots in 5 1/2 x 30 in. pieces and fasten with a round-head screw every 6 in. through top side. Lap each corner with 4 x 36 in. crosspieces, fasten with two flat-head screws. Fasten fiber glass to crosspieces with round-head screws and washers.

Then Assemble open-bottom coldframe box by fastening with flat-head screws. Drill 1/4 in. pilot holes 1 in. from the end and 1/8 in. from edge in each corner of face and back panel, and every 6 in. along outside edge.

Last Attach cover unit to base, fitting hinges 12 in. from each outside corner on inside edge of back and bottom of cover. Cover should fit flat on base when closed.

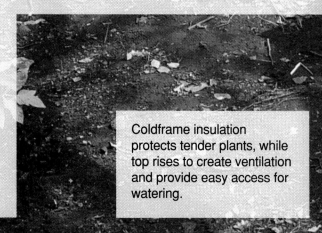

Coldframe insulation protects tender plants, while top rises to create ventilation and provide easy access for watering.

COLD FRAME MATERIALS

1 sheet 3/4 in. ABX plywood

1 26 x 30 in. piece white translucent fiber glass with corrugated ridges in 26 in. direction

2 2-in. galvanized metal butt hinges, with flat-head screws

36 1/4 x 1 1/4 in. flat-head, Phillips-head, brass or galvanized wood screws

18 1/2 x 1/8 in. galvanized washers

1 outdoor thermometer

HARDENING TRANSPLANTS

THE IMPORTANCE OF HARDENING

Hardening off is the process of acclimating seedlings started indoors to the outdoor environment by gradually increasing their exposure to bright sunlight and cooler outdoor temperatures. Adjusting plants to the outdoors a little each day can prevent the wilting, sunburned leaves and stunted growth caused by transplant shock. Hardening also helps to prepare the plant for the rigors of the outdoors, such as wind, rain, and sudden temperature changes.

Originally developed to aid northern gardeners in stretching the growing season, hardening off is now a recommended practice in all climates. Nursery-grown tomato plants are already hardened off and do not require this step.

Begin hardening off seedlings one week before transplanting outdoors. Harden off larger seedlings in the same flats or individual containers in which they were grown indoors. Move plants outdoors to a sheltered location, a coldframe, a shaded structure, or under a tree. Keep the flats off the ground to avoid insect damage. Soil in small containers will dry out quickly outdoors. Keep plants well watered during hardening. For the the first couple of days, place the plants in direct sun for 30 minutes to 2 hours and then move them back into the shade. During the next 2-3 days, gradually lengthen the exposure time to a half day of sun. Over the last 3 days, increase the exposure to a full day of sun. Each night, bring the plants back indoors or cover them to protect from chilly temperatures.

Open-Air Hardening

First Two weeks before transplanting, move plants outdoors. Gradually increase exposure to sun.

Then Shelter plants from direct sunlight and wind with a protective lath covering.

Next Keep plants watered. Wind and sun quickly rob plants of needed moisture.

Last After being in sun, move plants indoors or into shady area. Cover at night.

Coldframe Hardening

First Place tender plants in coldframe and close cover if frost is still likely.

Then Open coldframe for increasing periods during seasonally warm days.

Next Keep coldframe plants evenly watered at all times.

Last Close coldframe at night to protect plants from frost.

Planting Outdoors

The outdoor planting method to use depends on whether you are sowing seeds directly into garden soil or transplanting already-hardened seedlings. In either case, make sure the soil is turned over to a depth of 18-24 inches.

Before Planting

Before planting, make sure the danger of frost has passed and morning soil temperature is above 60°F, so seeds sprout without developing fungal diseases.

Soil should be damp and crumbly, not dry or sticky. Soil pressed in palm of hand should crumble to loose dirt. Rake planting area smooth and level before planting.

Planting Seeds in the Ground

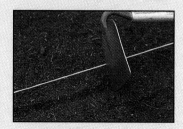

First Rake surface smooth, make row guide with strings and stakes and dig 1/4 in. deep furrows 2–3 ft. apart using hoe.

Then Place two or three seeds together in furrow, spacing seeds every 2 ft. down row.

Third Cover seeds with 1/4 in. of soil by closing sides of row and firming soil over seeds with fingers.

Last Keep seeded area damp until germination.

If possible, transplant on a cloudy day to prevent water stress and root shock.

Bury plants up to the first true leaves so the buried stem sends out more roots.

Planting Transplants

Either Tear away top of peat pot to stop it from wicking water away from plants, then plant whole pot beneath soil surface up to first true leaves.

Or Remove plant by holding container upside down and tapping gently to release rootball. Set rootball deep enough to bury plant up to first true leaves.

Last Cover with soil and firm ground around plant. Water around side of plant gently, adding half-strength liquid fertilizer. Keep soil moist until plant is well established.

41

THINNING AND SPACING

After transplants are established outdoors, continue to thin out the weaker plants.

If plants become leggy, they can be salvaged. Follow the steps at right to correct this common problem, which may be caused by overcrowding plants. If two seeds were started outdoors, two seedlings will usually grow. Snip off the smaller, weaker seedling at the base of the stem with scissors. Don't pull up a paired seedling by the stem as this may catch and damage the root system of the better plant. Thinning is important at this stage because, once established in the ground, plants compete for food and water and intertwine their roots as they grow.

Correct plant spacing depends on the type and variety of tomato. Full-size transplants should be spaced 18–36 inches apart. Miniature types can be planted closer together, but the sprawling indeterminate types may need as much as three feet between them eventually.

Smaller, weaker plants will look puny compared to their hardier siblings.

Replanting Leggy Plants

First Deepen or dig new hole at proper spacing and water with slow-release fertilizer in solution.

Then Lift out plant carefully using a small trowel. Cut soil around edge of rootball, if needed.

Third Pinch off first true leaves, bury plant up to second true leaves.

Last Firm soil by pressing earth down around rootball, then water lightly to settle. The buried stem will sprout additional roots.

Use small scissors to snip off weaker transplants at base of stem, taking care not to disturb neighboring plant.

GROWING IN CONTAINERS

Don't let a lack of garden space stop you from growing tomatoes. Simply choose a tomato variety suitable for growing in containers (see pg. 25) and a sunny spot to set the pot.

Planting in Containers

First Choose a sturdy wood, plastic or clay container, large enough for the variety being grown.

Then Fill container with sterilized soil; add peat moss to aid water absorption.

Third Dig a hole and bury the plant up to first true leaves.

Fourth Use a short stake secured to the stem with soft ties for support.

Next Soak plant with water to replenish roots. Water daily untill established.

Last Protect plant from temperature extremes by moving or covering.

CONTAINER CARE

Container gardening presents special demands because of the limited soil volume and drainage. Waterlogging can result from using containers with poor drainage. However, dry soil is the most common problem because the air on the outside of the container pulls moisture out of the soil through evaporation. Plastic containers tend to hold water longer than clay or wood, since the moisture only evaporates from the surface of the soil.

Soil in containers also dries out more quickly than garden soil because the plant's roots cannot reach down to tap into underground water. Regular watering is critical. If you have a number of containers, consider attaching a drip irrigation system to the outdoor faucet and installing a timer to regulate water flow.

Sprawling is a potential problem with container-grown tomatoes. Most container varieties are determinate plants of a limited mature size, but some indeterminate types like 'Yellow Pear' and 'Super Sweet 100 Hybrid' tend to sprawl out if not trained properly. To control sprawl, place a trellis behind the plant and attach the spreading stems to the bars.

Don't confuse containers for starting plants with containers for growing tomatoes; anything below the one-gallon size is too small for growing even miniature tomatoes to fruit.

MULCHING

Mulching benefits all vegetable gardens by conserving soil moisture, thereby reducing water use, preventing weed germination and moderating the soil temperature.

Mulching is beneficial against cold weather since it provides insulation to both the surface soil and the root system.

Mulching doesn't protect the upper plant, but it helps lengthen the growing season by retaining the heat in the soil underneath. Hay or wheatstraw, decomposed manure, peanut hulls, wood chips, sawdust and peat moss are just a few of the organic mulches now in widespread use. Spread the mulch around the plants once they have been established for a month or so, piling the material no more than six inches deep.

Mulch cloth is a commercially-made product designed to allow water to penetrate into the soil as well as prevent weeds from establishing. It is quite effective but can be expensive if you have a large garden. Black plastic sheeting, usually with a drip irrigation system running underneath, insulates the ground and keeps bottom leaves from touching the soil. The sheeting is spread out over the entire garden bed and holes are cut out for the individual plants prior to planting. A drip irrigation system prevents water from spattering on the leaves.

Organic Mulching Lay organic matter around plants to insulate the soil. Use organic mulch in summer when the soil is already warm.

Mulch Cloth Use a porous mulch cloth around tender plants.

Plastic Mulch Black or opaque plastic sheeting is the least expensive method. You may want to poke holes in the plastic to allow for air circulation.

Hot Cap Place a specially made paper or plastic cone over each plant during cold weather.

Water Insulation Plastic channels filled with water retain heat to keep air warm around plant.

Moving Indoors Take container plants inside during unseasonal weather.

SUDDEN COLD SNAPS

Despite your best efforts to plan the correct spring planting date, late frosts and cold snaps can happen. Unseasonal cold weather will kill or damage unprotected plants. Covering and mulching provide useful protection against light frosts. Unexpected cold snaps require more solid shelter. Among the outdoor insulation methods available are traditional hot caps, plastic bleach or water bottles with the bottoms cut off, vented row covers and cardboard boxes. Simply place the covering over and around the plant and leave it on until the cold spell has passed.

Severe cold spells require heavier insulation. Systems for insulating transplants include water-filled inner tubes that absorb and retain daytime heat and a commercial version of the same idea with channeled plastic tubes holding warm water around the plant. Ridged fiber glass panels can be arched over planted rows, with ends left open in the daytime for air circulation. Wrapping wire tomato cages in plastic will also protect plants against unusual wind and cold.

Almost anything that creates a miniature greenhouse for your transplants will improve their chances. With late snows, unprotected plants should be immediately covered with hay or burlap, so keep these materials handy in case of a cold snap with precipitation.

Staking and Caging

Using Vertical Space

Make the most of limited garden space by supporting your tomato plants vertically with stakes, wire cages, wooden lattices, trellises or overhead hooks and string. When harvest time comes, these open supports allow easy access for picking the fruit.

The type of vertical support to choose depends on which materials you prefer. Single 1 x 1 inch stakes about six to eight feet tall will support most indeterminate varieties well; plant the seedling on the south side at the stake's base. For giant or sprawling varieties, position four stakes like a box around the plant and support the stem and vines with string.

Wire cages offer fruit the best protection against sunscald (see pg. 63). Cone-shaped tomato cages are a standard garden shop and nursery item; a cylindrical tube of fencing about two feet across and five feet tall will do the same job. A wide variety of wooden lattice and trellis designs are available. The plants can be grown through the lattice or supported with wire mesh, twine or tape.

The objective of vertical support is to increase the amount of space for the stem to grow so that you increase the amount of fruit from each tomato plant.

You can also train the plant horizontally along a line of supports. Install a row or box pattern of stakes around your garden bed, run twine between the stakes about 12 inches from the ground and train the tomato stem to grow along the twine. Horizontal training keeps tomatoes off the ground and lessens the stooping if easy picking is your aim.

Single Stake   Tie the main stem of plant to a 6–8 ft., 1 x 1 in. wood stake.

Stake Box   Position four stakes around sprawling plants and support stems and vines with string.

Cone Cage   A conical wire cage maximizes fruit protection by holding branches and leaves outward.

Cylindrical Fence Encircle plants with wire fencing, threading branches through the wide mesh.

Lattice Wooden lattice freestanding or against a wall holds up plants.

Horizontal Training Any method that raises vines above ground helps keep plants healthy.

CONTROLLING GROWTH

Determinate plants rarely need pruning, and the blossoms on the ends of their vines should never be cut back. Indeterminate plants usually require some pinching and pruning to prevent sprawling and promote fruit development. There are three basic methods of pruning: single-stem, double-stem and multiple-stem. To grow a double-stem plant, allow the bottom sucker just below the first flower cluster to grow into a second main stem. To grow a multiple-stem plant, select three or four strong stems for maximum fruit production.

Pinch off suckers (the side shoots between the main stem and branches) to train the plant to a single stem. Pruning out small suckers once or twice a week will prevent indeterminate plants from sprawling or keeling over and reduce the number of vines needing support. Prune all lower branches with yellow or brown leaves. Cut shoots and branches flush with the stem. Pinch off the top of the main stem when the plant finally reaches the desired height.

Effective pruning always balances the need for good air circulation with the need for protective foliage and higher fruit yields. In dry, hot weather, avoid pruning back foliage so much that the fruit cracks or gets scalded by the sun. In humid or rainy climates, prune foliage back to avoid leaf rot. Always keep enough leaves for adequate photosynthesis and food development.

49

WATERING

THE PURPOSE OF WATERING

Proper watering is critical to good plant growth and high fruit yield, but there is no single watering schedule for all tomato plants everywhere. As a rule, slow and steady watering yields the best results.

The purpose of watering is not simply to provide moisture to the plants but also to assist in feeding the root system and plant. As water percolates downward through the soil, it carries minerals and micronutrients to be absorbed by the roots. Watering is particularly important for dissolving dry fertilizer, since granulated powders and pellets are useless if left lying on the soil surface (see pg. 52).

Like most vegetables, tomatoes prefer a consistent, regular supply of water for continuous growth. Unless the water penetrates below the surface to the deeper root system, roots will grow back up toward the surface and dry out when the topsoil gets hot in the daytime. These roots will feed poorly and eventually weaken the stem of the plant. In climates with rainy, humid summer seasons, on the other hand, plants may get all the moisture they need without any additional watering. You may even have to improve drainage in boggy soil where the water table is high.

A bubbler hose attachment keeps foliage dry and prevents plant damage caused by too much water all at once.

HOW TO WATER

Once your transplants are well established and their root systems can take up water from the surrounding earth, put them on a steady, even watering schedule that is adjusted to the soil moisture, drainage, humidity and air temperature of your garden. Always let the soil around established plants dry out between waterings.

If its leaves start to wilt from heat or dryness, the plant needs a good soaking at once. Avoid watering already-damp soil, because excess moisture waterlogs roots and encourages disease, particularly in heavy or poorly drained soil. If your garden has sandy, well-drained soil, you may need to water more often.

Many vegetable gardeners believe in daily watering, but mature tomatoes actually prefer less frequent heavy drenchings. Weekly waterings should be heavy enough to penetrate six inches or more into the soil. Dumping water on plants may damage stems and splash mud on bottom leaves, spreading soil-borne diseases. Instead, use a soaker or bubbler attachment and water around the plant's base.

Drip irrigation systems with automatic timers, available in garden stores, allow the steadiest, most controlled watering. Drip systems build up soil moisture slowly but surely. Be sure to shut off drip systems when it rains heavily during the growing season.

To prevent imbalanced growth, water should be evenly distributed around the plant and remain consistent from week to week. Mulching keeps moisture even and helps prevent radial cracking (see pg. 65) and susceptibility to disease.

FERTILIZING

Tomato plants are heavy feeders. Soil conditions and planting method determine fertilizer choice and application rates. Add fertilizer to the soil before transplanting, then sidedress around the plants when fruit sets. Feed plants regularly for the rest of the growing season.

Applying Dry Fertilizer

Either Apply granular mix directly by hand, 6–8 in. from plant stems.

Or Apply a composted material or manure as a fertilizing mulch.

Last Rake into top 1 in. of soil and water, repeating at regular intervals.

Applying Liquids or Mixes

Either Dilute liquid concentrate according to package directions.

Or Mix water-soluble powder in indicated proportions.

Last Moisten soil with plain water first, then pour fertilizer solution around base of plant.

Fertilizer Choices

Both organic and synthetic fertilizers will supply valuable nutrients to tomato plants. Many gardeners have been successful using synthetic dry or liquid fertilizers, while others prefer organic materials.

Organic fertilizers such as fish emulsion, bone meal, manure, wood ashes and compost are generally long-lasting, safe to use and will improve soil structure when mixed with native soil. Look for organic fertilizers that are well balanced in proportions of the three main nutrients—nitrogen (N), phosphorus (P) and potassium (K).

Synthetic fertilizers come premixed, with percentage by weight of nitrogen, phosphorus and potassium listed on the label along with application rates. Whether using a dry, dry-to-liquid or liquid mixture, apply any synthetic fertilizer carefully to avoid chemical burning of the plants. Always follow the directions on the label and water well after application.

Synthetics are best applied often and in small amounts, unless specifically formulated as timed-release agents that replace nitrogen steadily throughout the growing season.

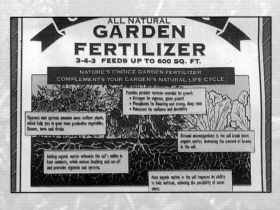

Use a hose-end sprayer to apply dry or liquid concentrates to plants; dilute with water according to label directions.

ORGANIC GARDENING

WEEDING

The most obvious of all gardening chores, weeding is also among the most important, whether you are growing tomatoes organically or not.

Weeds, when they appear, are always a problem, because they draw off soil nutrients and have a tendency to harbor pests and carry soil diseases. Most weed problems can be prevented without chemicals by practicing early maintenance. Let compost heat up to kill off weed seeds before application. Remove all plant debris when preparing the soil. Keep a good mulch on the soil during the spring growing season. Remove weeds before they go to seed.

Once the garden bed has been picked free of all weeds and the soil turned over, apply mulch between the young plants to prevent weeds from germinating in the soil. Weeding chores usually taper off once the tomato plants are full enough to shade the ground around them.

Weeding is only one of many soil surface maintenance tasks in the garden. Preventing leaves from touching the soil, cleaning up dead leaves and branches and keeping the ground around the plants clear are other important aspects of garden care.

Organic pest control methods are time-consuming but effective. Growing disease-resistant varieties is a good preventive measure. Proper weeding, pruning and mulching helps prevent pests and diseases.

HOW TO BE ORGANIC

Many people think organic gardening means growing without any artificial help, but the organic method includes a wide range of natural cultivation and fertilization techniques. Use of lime, sulfur and organic fertilizer is considered acceptable by most organic gardeners.

Organic gardening means more work at pest control and disease prevention, since chemical pesticides and fungicides are definitely unacceptable. Organic pest control involves picking off insects, slugs and snails by hand. If pests are too numerous to be hand-picked, use paper or aluminum collars and other traps against crawling bugs, or spray plants with soapy water. Pull up infected plants if necessary. Regularly turn over damp garden soil, and keep a compost pile going for soil amendment (see pg. 56). Seeding with modern disease-tolerant varieties enhances the organic garden's chance of success. A winter planting of *green manure* such as ryegrass or clover provides nitrogen when turned into the garden soil in spring. Add bone meal or rock phosphate for extra phosphorus just before installing plants. Use mulch to help control pests and soil diseases; later in the season, feed plants by mixing organic compost, well-rotted horse manure or other organic matter into the garden soil.

The organic garden needs more planning and maintenance than one where chemical pesticides and synthetic fertilizers are used, but it can produce fruit that are every bit as big and delicious.

Although organic fertilizers are natural, use care when applying them where pets and children have access. Disease prevention begins with proper soil preparation.

COMPOSTING

Adding compost to your tomato garden soil helps correct pH imbalances by neutralizing excess acidity or alkalinity. Compost also improves soil texture, aeration and percolation and recycles food and plant refuse.

COMPOST BOX MATERIALS

8 4 x 4 in. posts, 54 in. long

24 1 x 1 in. slot boards, 3 ft. long

44 2 x 6 in. side boards, 4 ft. long

Posthole concrete for 8 posts

1 box 3 in. nails

Building a Compost Box

First Assemble the construction materials and cut to length.

Then Dig postholes 18–24 in. deep. Set posts in concrete so that tops are 3 ft. above ground level.

Next Nail upright slot boards to posts with 2-in. gap. Fit 36 horizontal side boards into slots around perimeter.

Last Fit 4 side boards between each bin.

Making Compost

First Build up layers of plant debris and waste materials, avoiding toxic or disease-carrying items.

Next Aerate and water the half-composted pile, turning over the heated material regularly to speed decomposition.

Last Remove finished compost of a dark brown, crumbly texture and mix into garden soil.

USING COMPOST

You can compost from many organic materials—tree leaves, grass clippings, dead plants, sawdust, kitchen scraps and rotten fruit. Avoid tree leaves that are highly acid, such as oak leaves and pine needles, plants on which pesticides have been applied, any hay or grass that contains live seeds or sprigs and meat scraps or bones that will attract animals. Definitely leave out anything toxic or diseased.

Making compost is a simple process of building up layers of organic materials on top of each other. Once the pile is started, natural bacteria and earthworms go to work in the pile, heating it to 140–160° F and decomposing the ingredients into a rich, dark brown substance with the smell of freshly turned humus.

Aerification and watering ensure that the compost decomposes. Frequent watering speeds up the process. The fastest decomposition occurs with the addition of nitrogen and the use of mechanical turning devices such as drums. Compost must be turned every two or three days in order to decompose within a few months. One cubic foot of compost begins as four or five cubic feet of refuse, so build your compost pile to fit your garden size.

There are many commercially-made compost bins available, or follow these simple instructions to build one. Locate it for convenient use but out of sight of entertaining and play areas of the yard. Make compost throughout the year as a means of recycling. Use it throughout the yard. Turn the finished compost into the garden soil shortly before planting. Even if the compost doesn't add many new nutrients of its own, it will loosen the native soil and improve its drainage and texture.

PESTS

Different pests attack different parts of the fruit and foliage of the tomato plant. Each requires its own methods of control. Products available for controlling pests and diseases vary regionally. Knowing the enemy begins with identifying it and the kind of damage it causes.

Leafminers
Small wormlike flies, several generations per year. Maggots eat thin, winding paths through leaves. Defoliation or disease throughout growing season result. Control: spray or dust with appropriate pesticide.

Tomato Fruitworms
Caterpillar pest eats its way into fruit all season long. Common in the South and California. Control: dust before the insect reaches 1/2 in. long.

Potato Aphids
Common plant lice suck sap from underside of leaves. Spread by ants from plant to plant, many generations in a year. Control: wash with water, prune infested tips, use aluminum foil reflectors; spray serious infestations with appropriate pesticide.

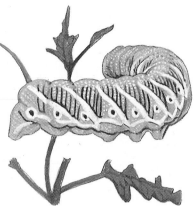

Hornworms
Large green 3–4 in. caterpillar; larvae eat foliage and fruit of the tomato plant. Two generations per year. Will consume large amounts of plant if left to feed. Control: handpick.

Whiteflies
Small, white-winged insects infest underside of new leaflets; discoloration, stunting and leaf drop result. Many broods in a year; difficult to control with insecticides or soaps. Control: introduce parasite *Encarsia formosa,* install yellow sticky traps.

Flea Beetles
Tiny, yellow-striped black insects, one or two generations annually. Attack the leaves of seedlings and thrive on any weeds in garden area, chewing small holes in leaves and helping transmit diseases. Control: dust with appropriate pesticide at time of transplanting.

Colorado Potato Beetles
Large 1–1 1/2 in. yellow beetle, one to three generations per year. Feeds on plant leaves throughout growing season, causes defoliation in seedlings. Control: handpick or dust.

Cutworms

1–2 in. caterpillar larvae, one to five generations annually. Destructive night feeder breaks off seedlings and young transplants. Control: clean plant debris in fall, turn over soil in spring, place barriers around transplants, apply appropriate pesticide if infestation is heavy.

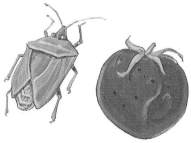

Stink Bugs

Brown (eastern, western U.S.) and green (Southeast) 1/2 in. long. Draws juice out of green or ripening fruit late in the season, deforms fruit, ruins textures. Control: clear weeds, apply appropriate pesticide.

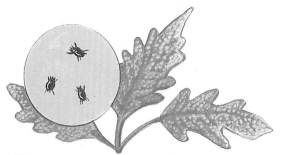

Mites

Tiny spider-like creatures, many generations per year. Feeds on leaves and fruit, causing leaf curling, yellowing and deformed fruit. Control: wash plant with a sharp spray of cold water.

CONTROLLING PESTS

Infestations of harmful pests can be very damaging to tomato crops; look for and combat them throughout the growing season. The first step is inspection and identification; learn to recognize the beneficial creatures, such as the ladybug and praying mantis, which should be left to flourish. Use the drawings at left to identify common pests.

The second step is removal. To block access, construct cardboard or aluminum foil barriers around the base of plant stems. Angle barriers downward and outward to make it hard for pests to crawl over. Pick off larger bugs and worms. Control smaller pests by spraying with water or washing with a soap-based insecticide. Take care not to damage small transplants or knock blossoms off flowering plants.

Serious infestations require the use of vegetable garden pesticides. Commercial pesticides come as powders for topical dusting, liquids for spraying or granular crystals for trench fumigation. Dusting from a can is easiest; liquids need to be mixed to correct proportions before spraying. Trench fumigation, or digging and pouring pesticide into the soil, is the most involved procedure. This method kills burrowing pests that hide in the soil to avoid dusts and sprays.

CAUTION

Use care with all pesticides applied to fruits and vegetables; follow manufacturer's directions carefully and use only as indicated.

DISEASES

Gray Leaf Spot
Stemphylium species

Common fungus in Southeast, causes dark brown spots on underside of leaves, followed by large holes and eventual defoliation. Carried by dead plant debris in soil and airborne spores. Control: rotate crops, apply fungicide, remove infected plants.

Late Blight
Phytophthora species

Fungus causing green-black patches on leaf edges, followed by mold growth, loss of leaves and fruit rot. Spread by spores during humid weather with cool nights. Control: remove infected plants, spray or dust.

Septoria Leaf Spot
Septoria species

Wet weather fungus common in mid-Atlantic region, shows small gray spots on leaves as plants set fruit, later defoliation and sunscalding. Spores spread by infected plant debris, rain splashing or hand contact. Control: sterilize soil, spray with fungicide, resistant varieties.

Early Blight
Alternaria species

Humid climate fungus also called *alternaria* leaf spot, infests plants in spring. Shows circular, dark brown spots on mature leaves, may become sunken areas at stem. Caused by excess dew or poor drainage. Control: remove infected plants, apply fungicide.

Bacterial Canker
Corynebacterium species

Seed-borne bacteria, shows light streaks on the stem and under branches; fruit are small and may have darkish holes. Spread by seeds and carried in soil. Control: clean seeds, rotate plants, sterilize soil.

Anthrachose
Colletotrichum species

Fungus occurring in hot, humid weather, showing circular, water-soaked spots on ripe fruit. Persists in soil and infests healthy plants in spring. Caused by rain splashing, poor drainage. Control: rotate soil, remove infected plants, dust.

Bacterial Spot
Xanthomonas species

Small dark bacterial spots on leaflets, followed by blossom drop and infection of mature leaves. Spread by leaf wounds, excess dampness, windy rainstorms. Control: clean seeds and seedlings.

Verticillium Wilt
Verticillium species

Common fungus causes wilting followed by yellowing of leaves and defoliation. Spore is carried from infected soil, prefers temperatures of 70–75°F. Control: sterilize soil, rotate crops, spray with fungicide, resistant varieties.

Fusarium Wilt
Fusarium species

Soil-borne virus, shows drooping and yellowing of leaves from base up. Most serious where soil temperature is over 80°F. Spread by contaminated soil. Control: sterilize soil, use resistant varieties.

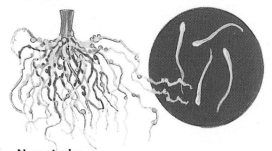

Nematodes
Meloidogyne species

Common eelworm pest, attacking roots of plant to cause root knots, stunting and wilting. Control: fumigate, use resistant varieties.

Tobacco Mosaic Virus

Common virus attacks members of nightshade family; shows green or yellow mottling of foliage, followed by leaf curling and brown spots on fruit. Found in tobacco and on smoker's hands, spread by contact. Control: wash hands carefully, use resistant varieties.

PREVENTION AND CONTROL

Depending on where you garden, tomato diseases are subject to a greater or lesser degree of control. In greenhouses, outdoor containers, planter boxes or sterilized hotbeds where heat is also used to kill microorganisms, most diseases can be avoided by using new potting soil. In poorly drained or overly humid garden beds, however, you may have to rotate crops, burn infected plants and spray or dust with fungicides in order to control disease.

Disease prevention is most easily accomplished before planting through the selection of disease-resistant and disease-tolerant varieties. Use only clean, guaranteed seeds, and inspect all purchased plants carefully; bacterial and fungal diseases can cause more damage to the plants they spread to than to the plant first contaminated.

Many tomato diseases are caused by poor soil or climate conditions, and prevention by seed selection is not possible. Good soil preparation, proper drainage and watering and regular feeding are needed to prevent and control these diseases. Where soil-borne bacteria such as bacterial canker or fungi such as late blight prove persistent, you have to remove all infected plants. Crop rotation may not eliminate these diseases if water run-off carries infected soil from one area of the garden to another.

COMMON PROBLEMS

Many of the ailments that afflict tomatoes are physiological in nature. Inspect plants closely for signs of problems caused by uneven watering, over-fertilizing or loss of foliage.

BLOSSOM DROP Low soil moisture, cold or hot spells, or over-feeding inhibit pollination and cause blossoms to fall off.

POOR POLLINATION Gentle shaking aids pollination; tap the flowers lightly on a warm, sunny day between 10 a.m. and 2 p.m.

LACK OF FRUIT An abundance of fruit should set after proper pollination occurs. If none appears, try tapping flowers; move container grown plants closer together.

Catface Disturbance or injury to the flowers causes scars, puckering and disfigurement at the blossom end of the growing fruit.

Sunscald Loss of protective foliage around green fruit during hot, dry weather, pests or diseases that reduce foliage cause overexposure.

Blossom End Rot Uneven water supply or excess nitrogen prevent the plant from taking up calcium, causing large dark spots at the blossom end of the growing fruit.

GOOD GARDENING PRACTICES

AVOIDING COMMON MISTAKES

The common mistakes many gardeners make involve spacing, watering, feeding and cleaning the garden. A little extra effort in these areas goes a long way toward preventing growing problems.

Avoid growing plants too close together. Although tomatoes take up little space, their roots require enough soil volume to hold adequate nutrients. If your plants are too close, thin them out by snipping off the unwanted plants. Pulling them up might damage the roots of remaining plants.

It is easy to tell when a plant is not getting enough water, as it wilts. Over-watering is harder to spot; look for leaf roll and blackened stems and tips. Correct over-watering by removing mulch to let soil dry out and cutting back on water.

Test your garden soil for natural nutrients before fertilizing, and always add fertilizer in the proper amounts. To correct over-fertilizing, water heavily to leach fertilizer through the soil and wait an extra week to resume fertilizing schedule.

Keeping the soil surface clean and pruning off bottom leaves that touch the ground or neighboring plants help prevent rotting fruit and leaf material from providing a home to the pests and diseases that prey on tomato plants.

Avoid overcrowding plants by spacing them properly, thinning when needed and pruning excess side and bottom foliage.

Pale Leaves Lack of basic soil nutrients causes pale, drooping leaves and poor fruiting; amend soil as needed (see pg. 52).

Fruit Rot Contact between the ground and fruit causes rotting; prune off bottom leaves and keep fruit high and dry.

Heavy Foliage Over-fertilizing with nitrogen greens up the leaves but also inhibits flower and fruit development.

Leaf Roll Over-watering or poor drainage causes leaf roll, which can occur without obvious yellowing or spotting.

Cracking Radial cracking results from uneven or spotty watering, causing the growth rate of the fruit to fluctuate.

Wilting Under-watering causes wilting, especially with new seedlings and transplants; water slowly and deeply to reach the roots.

RIPENING AND PICKING

VINE RIPENED

All the care in nurturing the plant and its fruit—watering, feeding, training and soil cultivation—is rewarded when you pick a perfect, vine-ripened tomato.

Whichever tomatoes you choose to grow, full ripeness is the surest guarantee of juicy, tasty results.

Commercial growers consider a tomato to be ripe when the first signs of pinkness appear at the blossom end of the fruit. Home gardeners have the luxury of waiting until the entire fruit is a deep, rich color. Wait to pick the fruit until the flesh starts to soften slightly and the skin has a bright, glossy color. Holding the vine securely, carefully pluck the ripened fruit from the plant.

The tastiness of any home-grown tomato depends mostly on the variety and the stage of ripeness of the fruit. Oddly enough, the color of the fruit is not always the surest indicator of ripeness, although most red varieties deepen in color as ripening increases pigmentation.

Tomatoes have their highest sugar content after converting starches to sugar through the night. Pick the fruit in the morning for the best taste. Many tomato fanciers cannot resist eating their crop fresh off the vine, and most fully ripe tomatoes are so soft and delicate that this may actually be the surest guarantee against bruising and spoilage. Once picked, vine-ripened tomatoes will keep for weeks in a cool, dark pantry or closet between 65 and 70°F. Never refrigerate tomatoes.

PICKED GREEN

Green tomatoes should never go unpicked. Every tomato gardener has a crop of green tomatoes at the end of the season, if only a few fruit on each plant. Even when a whole plant fails to ripen at harvest, the green fruit can be used. Sliced and fried in batter, green tomatoes are a popular delicacy.

Pick large green tomatoes and store them indoors at or just below room temperature—approximately 68°F. Don't place them in direct sunlight or in the refrigerator. Tomatoes need to be in room temperature conditions to ripen properly, a process that takes several weeks. You can fool green tomatoes into ripening by wrapping them in newspaper or a brown paper bag; the ethylene gases emitted by the fruit and caught in the bag speed up ripening.

Fresh-picked tomatoes, whether green or not, won't ripen further below 50°F or keep well above 80°F, so don't refrigerate them or leave them sitting out in direct sun too long.

EXTENDING THE HARVEST

SPRING PLANNING

For a longer tomato season, plan ahead. Choose different types of tomatoes that will ripen and mature at different times. Time the transplanting of determinate varieties so that they reach maturity one after the other, over a long harvest period.

Mark the date and variety of each batch of seedlings when you transplant them outdoors. The "days to fruit" listed on the charts in this book (see pgs. 18–27) indicate the number of days from planting transplants outdoors until you can expect to harvest the fruit of your labor. However, the number of days to maturity won't be the same for every garden location. You can sometimes extend the harvest by placing identical plants in different garden areas. The ones that get more sunlight, warmth and soil nutrients will invariably ripen first.

The key to keeping tomatoes ripening on the vine during early autumn frosts is to have cold protection ready (see pg. 46). Late season varieties will continue bearing fruit at the end of the season. The longer tomatoes ripen, the more time they have to develop the sugars and acids that spell rich flavor.

Gardeners in the Deep South or Southwest can sometimes start a second crop of tomatoes in mid to late summer and harvest them until the winter holidays. In fact, the inventive indoor gardener can grow specially adapted greenhouse *forcing* varieties 365 days a year.

Autumn Protection

First Place organic mulching around the base of fruit-bearing plants to protect roots from early frost, disease and dampness.

Either Cover plants with plastic sheeting as protection from light frost.

Or Use row cover tents to protect at night, uncovering plants during remaining sunny days.

GROWING HERBS WITH TOMATOES

Many herbs and salad vegetables flourish in the same conditions you've established for tomatoes, allowing you to grow entire meals in your backyard.

THE COOK GARDENS

Growing herbs along with your tomatoes enables you to bring in a mixed harvest of salad vegetables and herbs that go together perfectly on the dining table.

Like tomatoes, most herbs grow best in well-drained soil. The ideal site is a gentle incline with sandy soil. However, herbs can be grown in containers indoors or out. Although individual herbs vary, most require a site that has full sunlight for five hours a day. Grow herbs from seed or purchase transplants at a nursery or garden center. Plant your companion herbs so they will come to maturity around the same time as your tomatoes.

Growing herbs alongside tomatoes guarantees you a good supply of fresh accent flavors for your fruit. Among the favorite companion herbs for tomatoes are basil, marjoram, oregano, cilantro and parsley. Fresh sweet basil leaves are particularly delicious on sliced tomatoes; chopped basil can also serve as a tomato salad garnish or as the main ingredient in Italian pesto sauce.

Marjoram and oregano can also be used to sprinkle on sliced eating tomatoes or as garnishes or flavorings in tomato dishes. Cilantro works well on sliced fresh tomatoes and on tomato-based salads. Parsley can be used either as a decorative garnish or as a stewing herb in tomato sauces.

All of these herbs add flavor and variety to the basic tomato taste; don't be afraid to try something different.

FREEZING AND CANNING

For year-round consumption, preserve your surplus tomato crop by freezing or canning. Canning takes more effort, but it conserves the fresh tomato flavor better.

For cold-pack canning, wash and peel fresh, ripe tomatoes. With your supply of clean jars, rings and lids at the ready, drop the tomatoes into jars, pressing down to fill the air space. Fill each jar within one-half inch of the top, add a teaspoon of salt and wipe the rim clean. Attach the lid with the rim sealed and screw the ring down tight. Place the filled jars in a boiling water bath, making sure they are covered with at least one inch of water, and boil for 45–50 minutes.

Hot-pack canning follows nearly the same procedure. Wash, peel and quarter ripe tomatoes, then boil the open jars for 35–40 minutes to about 170°F. More tomatoes fit into each jar this way, since they shrink in cooking, but the tomatoes lose some of their shape, flavor and texture in the process.

The simplest way to preserve tomatoes is to wash them carefully, pack them in plastic containers or freezer bags, and freeze them. As with canning, remove any air pockets from the bottom and leave a head space at the top of the container.

Label and date the jar or bag for future reference; frozen or canned tomatoes will keep 12 months if properly sealed and stored.

◆ CAUTION

Always keep jars, lids and rings sterile; never unscrew or retighten sealed jars; check seals after 12 hours.

Consult your Agricultural Extension Service if unsure about safety procedures.

SUN-DRIED TOMATOES

Another good way to preserve tomatoes is by sun-drying. Sun-dried tomatoes make a chewy, flavorful snack, topping for hors-d'oeuvres or condiment for salads and stir-fry dishes. Beefsteak and paste varieties are good for this process.

You'll need a dry, sunny outdoor surface, screened off from insects. Clean and quarter the tomatoes, then blanch them in boiling water for three to five minutes. Strain out loose skins and seeds and press out any remaining water. Spread the sectioned fruit on trays and set outdoors. Turn tomatoes daily until dried.

If the weather is too humid, dry tomatoes indoors. Section and prepare as described above, then place the trays on a sunny windowsill or porch. To oven-dry, place trays in a 140–150°F oven for 6–12 hours, leaving the oven door slightly ajar. Commercial air driers or homemade driers with lightbulbs also work for drying tomatoes, as long as the temperature is kept moderate and air circulation maintained.

When the tomato sections are brittle and thoroughly dehydrated, remove them from the trays and pack them in airtight containers. Store sun-dried tomatoes in a cool, dark place, or refrigerate them if the weather gets very hot and humid.

CANNING EQUIPMENT
Jars and lids should be sterilized before use.

73

ENJOYING TOMATOES

After all is said and done, the real reward for growing tomatoes is in the eating. The versatile tomato can be enjoyed in many forms, allowing the harvest to brighten your meals through the year.

GREEN TOMATO PIE The tart green flavor is superb when baked in a pie.

TOMATO SAUCE A basic staple of the kitchen, served on pasta dishes.

SLICED TOMATOES Serve fresh with capers or other condiments and herbs.

TOMATO JUICE Drink it hot, cold or as a healthful, delicious soup.

SPICY SALSA Chopped tomatoes with onion, cilantro and pepper.

THE GARDENER COOKS

The complete kitchen garden produces a cornucopia of crisp vegetables and ripe tomatoes, from which the cook can prepare a limitless number of dishes. If you have successfully preserved all of your surplus tomato crop, you will never be without the ingredients for the many delicious recipes found in any cookbook.

Every cook should keep a good supply of tomato sauce on hand, for preparation of soups, stews, sauces and more exotic dishes. Frozen and canned tomatoes will meet your stewing, baking and pureeing needs long after the last fresh tomato has been picked from the vine.

Remember, preserved tomatoes make great gifts for nongardeners. The old wives' tale warning about too much acid in some tomatoes is no longer given much credence, so don't worry whether a particular variety has low or high acidity. All tomatoes lie within the middle pH range of natural food products and are less acidic than applesauce, peaches or cherries.

Tomatoes are a terrific source of vitamins C and A and lose little of their nutritional value when preserved, stored and cooked later. Whether preparing a warm red tomato soup or a tart green tomato pie, avoid cooking the tomatoes too long—all the flavor, texture and color can be lost by overcooking.

Properly prepared, home-grown tomatoes retain all the rich aroma and succulence of the fruit on the vine.

AGRICULTURAL EXTENSION

Each state's land grant university has a school or college of agriculture. Not all of these schools perform soil tests for the public, but any of them can refer you to your local agricultural extension service, available in every county in the United States. Nursery and garden stores can be easily found in the Yellow Pages. If you have further questions concerning federal or state programs in your area, call the U.S. Department of Agriculture Switchboard at 202-720-USDA.

State University Agricultural Extension Services:

ALABAMA Auburn University, Auburn, AL 36849 Telephone: (205) 844-4000

ALASKA University of Alaska, Fairbanks, AK 99775 Telephone: (907) 474-7211

ARIZONA University of Arizona, Tucson, AZ 85721 Telephone: (602) 621-2211

ARKANSAS University of Arkansas, Fayetteville, AR 72701 Telephone: (501) 575-2000

CALIFORNIA University of California, Berkeley, CA 94612 Telephone: (510) 987-0040

University of California, Davis, CA 95616 Telephone: (916) 752-1011

University of California, Riverside, CA 92521 Telephone: (714) 787-1012

COLORADO University of Colorado, Fort Collins, CO 80523 Telephone: (303) 491-1101

CONNECTICUT University of Connecticut, Storrs, CT 06269 Telephone: (203) 486-2000

DELAWARE University of Delaware, Newark, DE 19716 Telephone: (302) 735-8200

DISTRICT OF COLUMBIA University of the District of Columbia, Washington, D.C. 20008 Telephone: (202) 282-7300

FLORIDA University of Florida, Gainesville, FL 32611 Telephone: (904) 392-3261

GEORGIA University of Georgia, Athens, GA 30602 Telephone: (706) 542-3030

HAWAII University of Hawaii, Honolulu, HI 96822 Telephone: (808) 956-8111

IDAHO University of Idaho, Moscow, ID 83843 Telephone: (208) 885-6111

ILLINOIS University of Illinois, Urbana, IL 61801 Telephone: (217) 333-1000

INDIANA Purdue University, Lafayette, IN 47907 Telephone: (317) 494-4600

IOWA Iowa State University, Ames, IA 50011 Telephone: (515) 294-4111

KANSAS Kansas State University, Manhattan, KS 66506 Telephone: (913) 532-6011

KENTUCKY University of Kentucky, Lexington, KY 40506 Telephone: (606) 257-9000

LOUISIANA Louisiana State University, Baton Rouge, LA 70803 Telephone: (504) 388-3202

MAINE University of Maine, Orono, ME 04469 Telephone: (207) 581-1110

MARYLAND University of Maryland, College Park, MD 20742 Telephone: (301) 405-1000

MASSACHUSETTS University of Massachusetts, Amherst, MA 01003 Telephone: (413) 545-0111

MICHIGAN Michigan State University, East Lansing, MI 48824 Telephone: (517) 355-1855

MINNESOTA University of Minnesota, St. Paul, MN 55455 Telephone: (612) 625-5000

MISSISSIPPI Mississippi State University, MS 39762 Telephone: (601) 325-2131

MISSOURI University of Missouri, Columbia, MO 65211 Telephone: (314) 882-2121

MONTANA Montana State University, Bozeman, MT 59717 Telephone: (406) 994-0211

NEBRASKA University of Nebraska, Lincoln, NE 68503 Telephone: (402) 472-7211

NEVADA University of Nevada-Reno, Reno, NV 89557 Telephone: (702) 784-6611

NEW HAMPSHIRE University of New Hampshire, Durham, NH 03824 Telephone: (603) 862-1234

NEW JERSEY Rutgers University, New Brunswick, NJ 08903 Telephone: (908) 932-1766

NEW MEXICO New Mexico State University, Las Cruces, NM 88003 Telephone: (505) 646-0111

NEW YORK Cornell University, Ithaca, NY 14853 Telephone: (607) 255-2000

NORTH CAROLINA Duke University, Durham, NC 27706 Telephone: (919) 684-2135

NORTH DAKOTA North Dakota State University, Fargo, ND 58105 Telephone: (701) 237-8011

OHIO Ohio State University, Columbus, OH 43210 Telephone: (614) 292-6446

OKLAHOMA Oklahoma State University, Stillwater, OK 74708 Telephone: (405) 744-5000

OREGON Oregon State University, Corvallis, OR 97331 Telephone: (503) 737-0123

PENNSYLVANIA Pennsylvania State University, University Park, PA 16802 Telephone: (814) 865-4700

PUERTO RICO University of Puerto Rico, Mayaguez, PR 00681 Telephone: (809) 832-4040

RHODE ISLAND University of Rhode Island, Kingston, RI 02881 Telephone: (401) 792-1000

SOUTH CAROLINA Clemson University, Clemson, SC 29634 Telephone: (803) 656-3311

SOUTH DAKOTA South Dakota State University, Brookings, SD 57007 Telephone: (605) 688-4151

TENNESSEE University of Tennessee, Knoxville, TN 37916 Telephone: (615) 974-1000

TEXAS Texas A & M University, College Station, TX 77843 Telephone: (409) 845-4747

Texas Technological University, Lubbock, TX 79409 Telephone: (806) 742-2808

UTAH Utah State University, Logan, UT 84322 Telephone: (801) 750-1000

VERMONT University of Vermont, Burlington, VT 05405 Telephone: (802) 656-3131

VIRGINIA Virginia Polytechnic Institute, Blacksburg, VA 24061 Telephone: (703) 231-6000

WASHINGTON Washington State University, Pullman, WA 99164 Telephone: (509) 335-3564

WEST VIRGINIA University of West Virginia, Morgantown, WV 26506 Telephone: (304) 293-0111

WISCONSIN University of Wisconsin, Madison, WI 53706 Telephone: (608) 262-1234

WYOMING University of Wyoming, Laramie, WY 82070 Telephone: (307) 766-4133

INDEX

A Note From
NK Lawn and Garden Co.

For more than 100 years, since its founding in Minneapolis, Minnesota, NK Lawn and Garden has provided gardeners with the finest quality seed and other garden products.

We doubt that our leaders, Jesse E. Northrup and Preston King, would recognize their seed company today, but gardeners everywhere in the U.S. still rely on NK Lawn and Garden's knowledge and experience at planting time.

We are pleased to be able to share this practical experience with you through this ongoing series of easy-to-use gardening books.

Here you'll find hundreds of years of gardening experience distilled into easy-to-understand text and step-by-step pictures. Every popular gardening subject is included.

As you use the information in these books, we hope you'll also try our lawn and garden products. They're available at your local garden retailer.

There's nothing more satisfying than a successful, beautiful garden. There's something special about the color of blooming flowers and the flavor of home-grown garden vegetables.

We understand how special you feel about growing things—and NK Lawn and Garden feels the same way, too. After all, we've been a friend to gardeners everywhere since 1884.